LIFE PICTURE PUZZLE

WELCOME TO LIFE'S TENTH
PICTURE PUZZLE BOOK

Here we are, less than five years after publishing our first Picture Puzzle book, and we find ourselves already at our 10th! We'll be honest: When we invented these puzzle books we never expected that the response would be so overwhelming that we might have to keep the presses running—and our puzzle masters hard at work—almost constantly. But the letters and e-mails keep pouring in, asking for more puzzles. We're only too happy to comply: These Picture Puzzle books are fun to work on. And now we have 10.

To celebrate this milestone, we figured we needed a big theme. We had already traveled across America in one book and looked at holidays in another, dealt with animals in a third, and, in our last volume, presented a book's worth of mysteries drawn from old movies and TV shows. What now, for big No. 10? Well, why not traverse the whole wide world?

And so we do, sailing the seven seas and visiting every hemisphere. We have brought changes to famous sites like the Eiffel Tower, seen on our cover, and to out-of-the-way secrets known only to the locals. As always, we have tried to choose the most vivid, most colorful, most fun photographs. This book will make any puzzle player happy, and it's also a cheerful travelogue.

Our 10th book captures what's best about the whole series, and everything you loved about our earlier books is still here. Our Novice section sets an easy pace so you can ramp up your skills as you go. Our Master and Expert sections incrementally add to the challenge, and when you tackle our Genius puzzles, you'll be a certified puzzle master yourself.

But you already knew all that. You're familiar with how our books proceed. You've been with us a long time now. Ten whole books.

And counting!

[OUR CUT-UP PUZZLES: EASY AS 1-2-3]

We snipped a photo into four or six pieces. Then we rearranged the pieces and numbered them.

Your mission: Beneath each cut-up puzzle, write the number of the piece in the box where it belongs.

Check the answer key at the back of the book to see what the reassembled image looks like.

[HOW TO PLAY THE PUZZLES]

Trading Places

In this market, you're sure to get blanket coverage

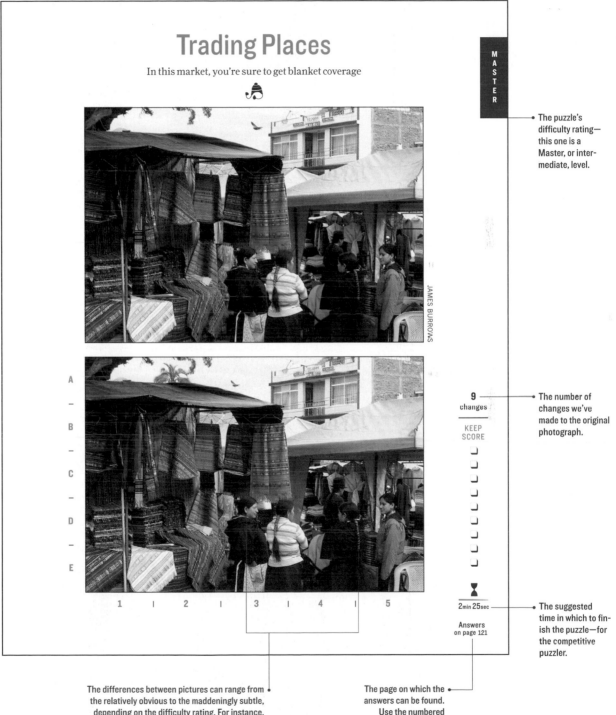

JAMES BURROWS

MASTER

The puzzle's difficulty rating—this one is a Master, or intermediate, level.

9 changes

The number of changes we've made to the original photograph.

KEEP SCORE

2min 25sec

The suggested time in which to finish the puzzle—for the competitive puzzler.

Answers on page 121

The differences between pictures can range from the relatively obvious to the maddeningly subtle, depending on the difficulty rating. For instance, one of these ladies has lost an earring, while another is sporting a braid of a different color. Seven more changes are left to spot in this puzzle.

The page on which the answers can be found. Use the numbered and lettered grid to help you find any changes you might have missed.

LIFE PICTURE PUZZLE

Puzzle Masters Forrester Hambrecht, Michael Roseman (Consulting)
Editor Robert Sullivan
Director of Photography Barbara Baker Burrows
Deputy Picture Editor Christina Lieberman
Creative Director Richard Baker
Copy Barbara Gogan (Chief), Danielle Dowling, Parlan McGaw
Writer/Reporter Marilyn Fu

LIFE Puzzle Books
Managing Editor Bill Shapiro

LIFE Books
President Andrew Blau
Business Manager Roger Adler
Business Development Manager Jeff Burak

Editorial Operations

Richard K. Prue (Director), Brian Fellows (Manager), Keith Aurelio, Charlotte Coco, John Goodman, Kevin Hart, Norma Jones, Mert Kerimoglu, Rosalie Khan, Patricia Koh, Marco Lau, Brian Mai, Po Fung Ng, Lorenzo Pace, Rudi Papiri, Robert Pizaro, Barry Pribula, Clara Renauro, Donald Schaedtler, Hia Tan, Vaune Trachtman, David Weiner

Time Inc. Home Entertainment
Publisher Richard Fraiman
General Manager Steven Sandonato
Executive Director, Marketing Services Carol Pittard
Director, Retail & Special Sales Tom Mifsud
Director, New Product Development Peter Harper
Assistant Director, Bookazine Marketing Laura Adam
Assistant Director, Brand Marketing Joy Butts
Associate Counsel Helen Wan
Book Production Manager Suzanne Janso
Design & Prepress Manager Anne-Michelle Gallero
Brand Manager Roshni Patel

Special thanks to Christine Austin, Jeremy Biloon, Glenn Buonocore, Jim Childs, Susan Chodakiewicz, Rose Cirrincione, Jacqueline Fitzgerald, Carrie Frazier, Lauren Hall, Jennifer Jacobs, Brynn Joyce, Mona Li, Robert Marasco, Amy Migliaccio, Brooke Reger, Dave Rozzelle, Ilene Schreider, Adriana Tierno, Alex Voznesenskiy, Sydney Webber, Jonathan White

PUBLISHED BY

LIFE Books

Vol. 10, No. 4 • June 11, 2010

Copyright 2010
Time Inc.
1271 Avenue of the Americas
New York, NY 10020

We welcome your comments and suggestions about LIFE Books. Please write to us at:
LIFE Books
Attention: Book Editors
PO Box 11016
Des Moines, IA 50336-1016

If you would like to order any of our hardcover Collector's Edition books, please call us at 1-800-327-6388 (Monday through Friday, 7 a.m. to 8 p.m., or Saturday, 7 a.m. to 6 p.m. Central Time).

COVER: CHROMACOME/GETTY

READY, SET,

GO!

CONTENTS

NOVICE	6
MASTER	42
EXPERT	78
GENIUS	94
CLASSICS	110
ANSWERS	120
JUST ONE MORE	128

NOVICE

[
These puzzles are for everyone:
rookies and veterans,
young and old. Start here, and
sharpen your skills.
]

Like Clockwork

Big Ben usually gets the time right three times out of four

DAN CHUNG/REUTERS/CORBIS

0min 35sec

Answer
on page 121

Way Beyond Frosty

Kids in Ottawa don't settle for snowmen

CARL & ANN PURCELL/CORBIS

A
B
C
D
E

1 2 3 4 5

8
changes

2min 10sec

Answers
on page 121

KEEP SCORE ★ ❑ ❑ ❑ ❑ ❑ ❑ ❑ ❑

Totally Digging Colorado

Will these archaeologists find any buried treasure at Shields Pueblo? Will you?

STEFANO AMANTINI/CORBIS

A
—
B
—
C
—
D
—
E

1   2   3   4   5

7
changes

2min 20sec

Answers
on page 121

KEEP SCORE ★ ❑ ❑ ❑ ❑ ❑ ❑ ❑

Pegasus

Pigs might not fly in England, but horses do

A
—
B
—
C
—
D
—
E

1   2   3   4   5

8
changes

2min 30sec

Answers
on page 121

KEEP SCORE ★ ❏ ❏ ❏ ❏ ❏ ❏ ❏ ❏

Frozen Dinner

At Japan's high-end Alpha Resort Tomamu, cold is hot

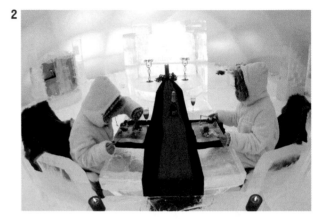

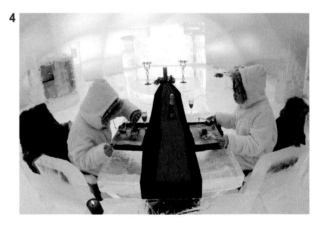

0min 55sec

Answer
on page 121

KIM KYUNG-HOON/REUTERS/CORBIS

Midday March

Which one of these photos has an off-color parade participant?

EMILY PRESCOTT

0min 45sec

Answer
on page 121

Rolling Along

In Newport Beach, California, Segway is *your* way

MICHELE & TOM GRIMM/CORBIS

A

B

C

D

E

1   2   3   4   5

7
changes

⧗

2min 25sec

Answers
on page 121

KEEP SCORE ★ ❑ ❑ ❑ ❑ ❑ ❑ ❑

Busman's Holiday

The tigers at Seoul's safari park want a look, too

PAUL CHESLEY/GETTY

A

B

C

D

E

1   2   3   4   5

8
changes

⧖

2min 30sec

Answers
on page 121

KEEP SCORE ★ ❑ ❑ ❑ ❑ ❑ ❑ ❑ ❑

Dutch Treat

This landscape is shifting with the wind

FABFOTO/GETTY

A
B
C
D
E

1   2   3   4   5

7
changes

⧗
2min**40**sec

Answers
on page 121

KEEP SCORE ★ ❑ ❑ ❑ ❑ ❑ ❑ ❑

Dracula Slept Here

In Romania, remember to *count* the changes. *Mwa-ha-ha!*

A

—

B

—

C

—

D

—

E

1   2   3   4   5

7
changes

3min 30sec

Answers
on page 122

KEEP SCORE ★ ❑ ❑ ❑ ❑ ❑ ❑ ❑

Do You Buy?

Nowadays in Dubai, the answer is probably "No"

A
—
B
—
C
—
D
—
E

1   2   3   4   5

7
changes

2min 5sec

Answers
on page 122

KEEP SCORE ★ ❏ ❏ ❏ ❏ ❏ ❏ ❏

Buzz Off

Flying insects on the beach in Perth can be such a nuisance

A
—
B
—
C
—
D
—
E

1   2   3   4   5

7
changes

⧗
1min 55sec

Answers
on page 122

KEEP SCORE ★ ❑ ❑ ❑ ❑ ❑ ❑ ❑

Head Over Heels

At Sea World in Australia, everyone's flippin'

8
changes

KEEP
SCORE!

☐
☐
☐
☐
☐
☐
☐
☐

⧗
2min 40sec

Answers
on page 122

Baaaah!

Life is woolly in Vermont

MELANIE STETSON FREEMAN/CHRISTIAN SCIENCE MONITOR/GETTY

A
—
B
—
C
—
D
—
E

1 | 2 | 3 | 4 | 5

8
changes

⧗
2min 15sec

Answers
on page 122

KEEP SCORE ★ ❏ ❏ ❏ ❏ ❏ ❏ ❏ ❏

The Sky's the Limit

Keep an eye on these rascally rockets in New Mexico

JOSE FUSTA RAGA/CORBIS

6
changes

⧗
1min 45sec

Answers
on page 122

KEEP SCORE ★ ❏ ❏ ❏ ❏ ❏ ❏

Where's Santa?

On the Russian Steppes, reindeer await the big guy's call

GERD LUDWIG/CORBIS

A

B

C

D

E

1   2   3   4   5

5
changes

⌛
1min 45sec

Answers
on page 122

KEEP SCORE ★ ❑ ❑ ❑ ❑ ❑

Making Merry

Camera phones are mandatory at Merryland in Guilin, China

A
—
B
—
C
—
D
—
E

1   2   3   4   5

8
changes

2min 05sec

Answers
on page 122

KEEP SCORE ★ ❏ ❏ ❏ ❏ ❏ ❏ ❏ ❏

Chillin' in Southern California

The penguins at San Diego's Sea World are on the march toward her magic chum bucket

KELLY-MOONEY/CORBIS

A

B

C

D

E

1   2   3   4   5

6
changes

⧗

2min 15sec

Answers
on page 122

KEEP SCORE ★ ❑ ❑ ❑ ❑ ❑ ❑

Olé

Can you spot the changes made to this bullring in Seville, Spain?

LUDOVIC MAISANT/HEMIS/CORBIS

A
B
C
D
E

1 2 3 4 5

6
changes

⏳
2min 55sec

Answers
on page 122

KEEP SCORE ★ ❑ ❑ ❑ ❑ ❑ ❑

MASTER

[
Here, puzzles get
a little harder. You'll
need to raise
your game a level.
]

Mirror Image

Everything's turned on its head in New York City

MARIO TAMA/GETTY

KEEP SCORE!

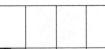

3min 10sec

Answers
on page 122

Getting a Leg Up

For these lovely lasses, it's sync or swim at London's Trafalgar Square

DANIEL BEREHULAK/GETTY

A

—

B

—

C

—

D

—

E

1 | 2 | 3 | 4 | 5

7
changes

⧗

2min 30sec

Answers
on page 123

KEEP SCORE ★ ❑ ❑ ❑ ❑ ❑ ❑ ❑

Here's Some Moore

A Henry Moore sculpture revamps the scene at Kew Gardens in England

A

—

B

—

C

—

D

—

E

1 | 2 | 3 | 4 | 5

10
changes

⧗

3min 15sec

Answers
on page 123

KEEP SCORE ★ ❑ ❑ ❑ ❑ ❑ ❑ ❑ ❑ ❑ ❑

Isn't It Good?

This harbor is full of boats made from Norwegian wood

PAWEL WYSOCKI/CORBIS

A
—
B
—
C
—
D
—
E

1   2   3   4   5

8
changes

⧗
2min 40sec

Answers
on page 123

KEEP SCORE ★ ❑ ❑ ❑ ❑ ❑ ❑ ❑ ❑

Pumpkin Pilot

Behold, Germany's giddy goddess of gourds

A
—
B
—
C
—
D
—
E

1 | 2 | 3 | 4 | 5

13
changes

⧗
3min 25sec

Answers
on page 123

KEEP SCORE ★ ❑ ❑ ❑ ❑ ❑ ❑ ❑ ❑ ❑ ❑ ❑ ❑ ❑

Ribbit

Dutch drivers will brake for giant frogs. Wouldn't you?

A —
B —
C —
D —
E

1 | 2 | 3 | 4 | 5

7
changes

⧗

2min 40sec

Answers
on page 123

KEEP SCORE ★ ❏ ❏ ❏ ❏ ❏ ❏ ❏

Pageantry in Prague

Find the differences among these Czechs, mate

A
—
B
—
C
—
D
—
E

1 | 2 | 3 | 4 | 5

9
changes

3min 50sec

Answers
on page 123

KEEP SCORE ★ ❑ ❑ ❑ ❑ ❑ ❑ ❑ ❑ ❑ ❑

Not So Grimm

You never know what will show up in this beautiful Black Forest backdrop

DAVE G. HOUSER/CORBIS

A

—

B

—

C

—

D

—

E

1 | 2 | 3 | 4 | 5

8
changes

2min 55sec

Answers
on page 123

KEEP SCORE ★ ❑ ❑ ❑ ❑ ❑ ❑ ❑ ❑

Puppy!

Well, no, my dear, things have changed

GETTY

A
–
B
–
C
–
D
–
E

1 2 3 4 5

8
changes

⏳
2min 40sec

Answers
on page 123

KEEP SCORE ★ ❑ ❑ ❑ ❑ ❑ ❑ ❑ ❑

Up, Up, and Away

Here's how the Swiss lift off

SANDRO VANNINI/CORBIS

9
changes

KEEP
SCORE!

⏳
3min 10sec

Answers
on page 124

PICTURE PUZZLE **LIFE** | **61**

Spanish Panache

In Barcelona, we made some un-Gaudi alterations

KEREN SU/GETTY

A — B — C — D — E

1   2   3   4   5

9
changes

⧗
3min 40sec

Answers
on page 124

KEEP SCORE ★ ☐ ☐ ☐ ☐ ☐ ☐ ☐ ☐ ☐

Slip Slidin' Away

Undergoing a transformation in the Middle East

1

2

3

4

5

6

1min 20sec

Answer
on page 124

MASSIMO BORCHI/ CORBIS

One Wired Pachyderm

In Sydney, a post-modern elephant you'll never forget

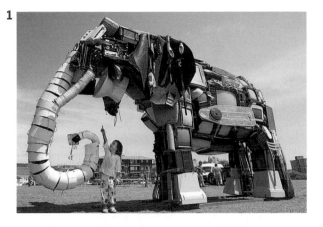

1

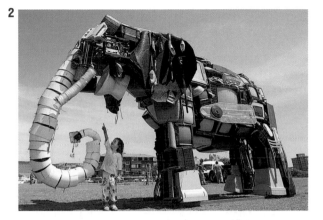

2

3

4

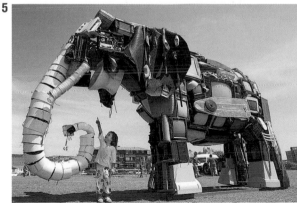

5

TORSTEN BLACKWOOD/AFP/GETTY

6

1min 35sec

Answer
on page 124

A Paddle Puzzle

Kayakers at Lake Tahoe face fluctuating conditions

A
—
B
—
C
—
D
—
E

1   2   3   4   5

9
changes

⏳

2min 20sec

Answers
on page 124

KEEP SCORE ★ ❑ ❑ ❑ ❑ ❑ ❑ ❑ ❑ ❑ ❑

Equine Elegance

These horses in Prague are dressed to impress

MICHAL CIZEK/AFP/GETTY

A
–
B
–
C
–
D
–
E

1   2   3   4   5

11
changes

4min 10sec

Answers
on page 124

KEEP SCORE ★ ❏ ❏ ❏ ❏ ❏ ❏ ❏ ❏ ❏ ❏ ❏

Mickey Slept Here

Take a peek through this mousehole at the Magic Kingdom.

ORJAN F. ELLINGVAG/DAGBLADET/CORBIS

A
—
B
—
C
—
D
—
E

1   2   3   4   5

10
changes

3min 30sec

Answers
on page 124

KEEP SCORE ★ ❏ ❏ ❏ ❏ ❏ ❏ ❏ ❏ ❏ ❏

Perplexing Pastoral

There are subtle secrets hidden here in Wales

A
—
B
—
C
—
D
—
E

1 | 2 | 3 | 4 | 5

12
changes

⏳

4min 20sec

Answers
on page 124

KEEP SCORE ★ ❑ ❑ ❑ ❑ ❑ ❑ ❑ ❑ ❑ ❑ ❑ ❑

Arms Up

It's high time to transform Tibet

TEH ENG KOON/AFP/GETTY

A
–
B
–
C
–
D
–
E

1   2   3   4   5

9
changes

⧗
3min 40sec

Answers
on page 124

KEEP SCORE ★ ❑ ❑ ❑ ❑ ❑ ❑ ❑ ❑ ❑

Bird's Eye View

What's old is new when you stroll down this Czech street

JON ARNOLD/GETTY

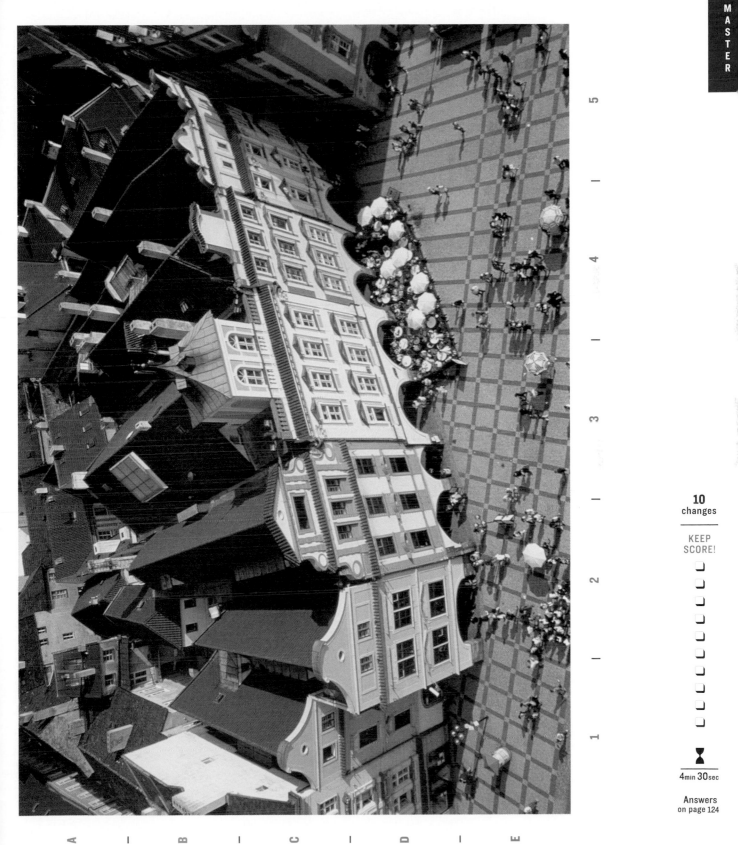

5

4

3

2

1

A

B

C

D

E

10
changes

KEEP
SCORE!

4min 30sec

Answers
on page 124

EXPERT

[
Only serious
puzzlers dare to
tread past this
point. Who's in?
]

Aspiring Spires

In Red Square, everything is on the up and up

HARALD SUND/GETTY

A
—
B
—
C
—
D
—
E

1   2   3   4   5

9
changes

KEEP
SCORE

⌛

4min 25sec

Answers
on page 125

Whoa!

Looks like they'll be changing this guard at Buckingham Palace

JIM WATSON/EPA/CORBIS

A
—
B
—
C
—
D
—
E

1   2   3   4   5

9
changes

3min 15sec

Answers
on page 125

KEEP SCORE ★ ❑ ❑ ❑ ❑ ❑ ❑ ❑ ❑ ❑ ❑

London Calling

And a daredevil has answered

RUNE HELLESTAD/CORBIS

A
—
B
—
C
—
D
—
E

1 | 2 | 3 | 4 | 5

9
changes

⌛

3min 35sec

Answers
on page 125

KEEP SCORE ★ ❑ ❑ ❑ ❑ ❑ ❑ ❑ ❑ ❑

Kayak Attack

What would Mark Twain make of this scene?

A
—
B
—
C
—
D
—
E

1   2   3   4   5

10 changes

⏳ 3min 55sec

Answers on page 125

KEEP SCORE ★ ❏ ❏ ❏ ❏ ❏ ❏ ❏ ❏ ❏ ❏

In Gay Paree

On a midsummer afternoon, everyone's ready for a cool drink

10
changes

KEEP
SCORE!

- [ ]
- [ ]
- [ ]
- [ ]
- [ ]
- [ ]
- [ ]
- [ ]
- [ ]
- [ ]

⏳
3min 40sec

Answers
on page 125

When in Venice . . .

. . . watch out for rising waters

MICHELE CROSERA/REUTERS/CORBIS

A

B

C

D

E

1   2   3   4   5

12
changes

⏳
4min 30sec

Answers
on page 125

KEEP SCORE ★ ❏ ❏ ❏ ❏ ❏ ❏ ❏ ❏ ❏ ❏ ❏ ❏

Morning Recess

Mind the madness among these Madrilenians

A

B

C

D

E

1   2   3   4   5

8
changes

⧖

3min 40sec

Answers
on page 125

KEEP SCORE ★ ❑ ❑ ❑ ❑ ❑ ❑ ❑ ❑

It Doesn't Quite Fit

In the Philippines, an Imelda reject (the only one)

1

2

3

4

5

6

1min 20sec

Answer
on page 125

ROMEO RANOCO/REUTERS/CORBIS

Savory Skewers

Which one of these cooks is less prepared to take your order?

1

2

3

4

5

6

JAMES BURROWS

1min 15sec

Answer
on page 125

GENIUS

[Finding a single difference
in these puzzles is a
challenge. Finding them all
might be impossible.]

O Canada

The Calgary Stampede Marching Band goes through a shifty town

GEORGE ROSE/GETTY

18
CHANGES

KEEP
SCORE!

☐
☐
☐
☐
☐
☐
☐
☐
☐
☐
☐
☐
☐
☐
☐
☐
☐
☐

⧗

5min 50sec

Answers
on page 126

A
—
B
—
C
—
D
—
E

1   2   3   4   5

The Fruity Nile

Someone's doling out fun in the sun in Egypt

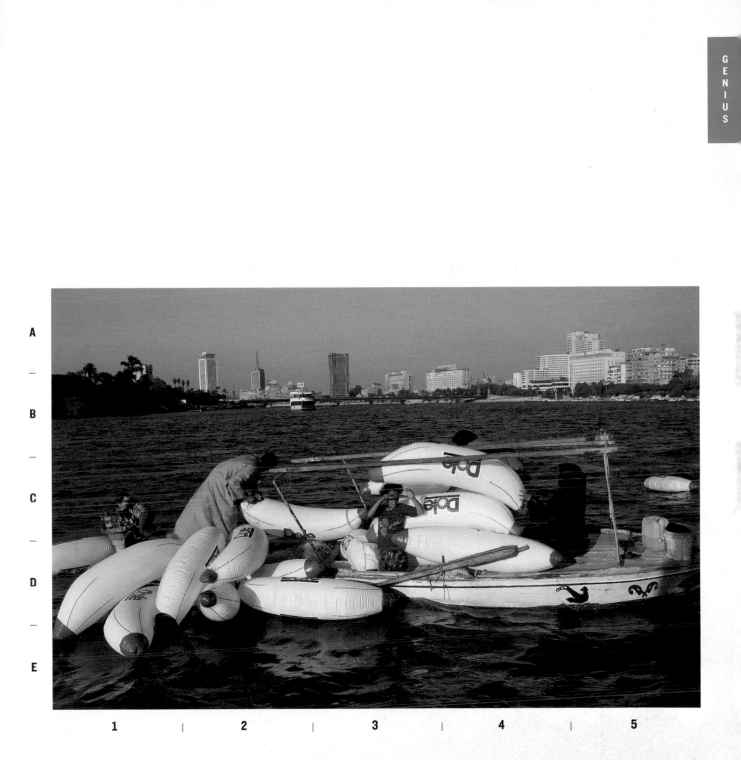

A
—
B
—
C
—
D
—
E

1   2   3   4   5

13
changes

4min 40sec

Answers
on page 126

KEEP SCORE ★ ❏ ❏ ❏ ❏ ❏ ❏ ❏ ❏ ❏ ❏ ❏ ❏ ❏

A Dab of India Ink

Final touches sometimes change everything

STRDEL/AFP/GETTY

19
CHANGES

KEEP
SCORE!

7min 50sec

Answers
on page 126

Let the Good Times Roll

It looks like this party is getting ready to take off

DAVID MCNEW/GETTY

A
—
B
—
C
—
D
—
E

1   2   3   4   5

18
changes

⧗
6min 10sec

Answers
on page 126

KEEP SCORE ★ ☐ ☐ ☐ ☐ ☐ ☐ ☐ ☐ ☐ ☐ ☐ ☐ ☐ ☐ ☐ ☐ ☐ ☐

Bali High

Reach out and touch someone

A
—
B
—
C
—
D
—
E

1   2   3   4   5

14
changes

⏳
5min **20**sec

Answers
on page 126

KEEP SCORE ★ ☐ ☐ ☐ ☐ ☐ ☐ ☐ ☐ ☐ ☐ ☐ ☐ ☐ ☐

You've Got Lemons . . .

. . . Make lemonade! Then solve this puzzle

A

B

C

D

E

1   2   3   4   5

11
changes

5min 20sec

Answers
on page 126

KEEP SCORE ★ ❑ ❑ ❑ ❑ ❑ ❑ ❑ ❑ ❑ ❑ ❑

To Kingdom, Come!

Mickey, Minnie, and friends are waiting

KELLY-MOONEY/CORBIS

A

B

C

D

E

1   2   3   4   5

15
CHANGES

KEEP
SCORE!

⌛

5min 40sec

Answers
on page 127

Water Taxis

Something's awry on this Venetian canal

1

2

3

4

5

6

⧗

3min 20sec

Answer
on page 127

STEFANO AMANTINI/CORBIS

String Theory

It might take a particle physicist to reassemble this colorful quartet

ELOY ALONSO/REUTERS/CORBIS

KEEP SCORE!

5min 20sec

Answer
on page 127

LIFE
CLASSICS

[These puzzles were
specially created with
memorable photos
from the LIFE archives.]

A Man, a Plan, a Canal

But we're in Italy, not Panama

DMITRI KESSEL

6
changes

KEEP
SCORE

⌛

3min 10sec

Answers
on page 127

Foxy Business

Once they've got the scent, these hounds will follow
the hunt through hill, dale, and even town

LARRY BURROWS

8
changes

KEEP
SCORE!

☐
☐
☐
☐
☐
☐
☐
☐

⏳
3min 30sec

Answers
on page 127

A Parisian Poseur

This Connecticut Yankee is spinning around
the City of Light and generally having the time of his life

GORDON PARKS

7
changes

⧗

3min 35sec

Answers
on page 127

KEEP SCORE ★ ❏ ❏ ❏ ❏ ❏ ❏ ❏

To the Manor Born

His is a noble steed indeed

MARK KAUFFMAN

A
–
B
–
C
–
D
–
E

1 | 2 | 3 | 4 | 5

6
changes

3min 5sec

Answers
on page 127

KEEP SCORE ★ ❏ ❏ ❏ ❏ ❏ ❏

Ain't It Grand!

Sure is, but watch out—the first step is a doozy

FRANK SCHERSCHEL

A
—
B
—
C
—
D
—
E

1 | 2 | 3 | 4 | 5

7
changes

3min 40sec

Answers
on page 127

KEEP SCORE ★ ❏ ❏ ❏ ❏ ❏ ❏ ❏

[ANSWERS]

Finished already? Let's see how you did.

[INTRODUCTION]

Page 3: Trading Places No. 1 (A2): Palm fronds gently peer down from above. No. 2 (A3): A pigeon confidently glides in for a landing. No. 3 (A4): It's as if that window had never existed. No. 4 (C2): This blanket is a lowrider. No. 5 (C4 to D4): The yellow canopy has lost half its support. No. 6 (C4): The hat is at least a quart too large. No. 7 (D3): She's going to be quite upset when she discovers her earring is missing. No. 8 (D4): Will you accept some pink blankets in lieu of the blue ones? No. 9 (D5): Her braid has gone through an amazing color transformation.

[NOVICE]

Page 7: Like Clockwork
In No. 3, 10 is the new 12.

Page 8: Way Beyond Frosty No. 1 (A4): The temperature must be rising because this chimney melted! No. 2 (B1): One tree less. No. 3 (B3): This time a whole building melted. No. 4 (B4 to C4): She just pulled a 180. No. 5 (C3): This child's hat has gone blue with the cold. No. 6 (C3 to D3): His hat no longer matches his friend's. No. 7 (D3): That boy's yellow stripe turned white. No. 8 (D4): Where'd his leg go?

Page 10: Totally Digging Colorado No. 1 (C1): Hello feline friend. No. 2 (C2): He looks better in pants. No. 3 (C2 to D2): Blue like the sky. No. 4 (D4): Buckets of fun. No. 5 (D1): Where did my spray bottle go? Someone got thirsty. No. 6 (E2): A bigger pad for production! No. 7 (E3 to E4): Whatever did happen to Jimmy Hoffa?

Page 12: Pegasus No. 1 (A3): Hey, you, get off of my cloud! No. 2 (A3 to B3): My, what big ears you have. No. 3 (B2): This bar better not fade away. No. 4 (D1): The race isn't over until the last song is sung. No. 5 (D2): You put your hind leg in and

then you shake it all about. No. 6 (D3): The white stripes ganged up to rub out the black stripe. No. 7 (D4 to E4): A lot of bolts have . . . bolted. No. 8 (E1 to E2): New panelling has been installed along the fence.

Page 14: Frozen Dinner
In No. 4, a candle has disappeared.

Page 15: Midday March
In No. 4, a member of the cavalcade has changed her skirt.

Page 16: Rolling Along No. 1 (A3): A palm has flipped its top. No. 2 (A4): West Coast sunshine can make just about anything grow faster—including a gangly old palm. No. 3 (C1): It's sure a nice day for boating, isn't it? No. 4 (C3): Every year on this day, she visits California just to stand at the water's edge and contemplate the sea. No. 5 (C4): Okay, who stole the electrical cabinet? No. 6 (C5): She donned a new T-shirt while you weren't looking. No. 7 (D1 to D2): A vampire casts no shadow.

Page 18: Busman's Holiday No. 1 (A2 to A3): Someone's getting ready for lunch. No. 2 (A3): He can't hide behind those sunglasses. No. 3 (B5): We've got a really, really big window for you. No. 4 (C1): The wheel is one bolt shy. No. 5 (C3): When did they convert the bus to all electric and ditch the gas tank? Nos. 6 and 7 (C4): The tiger glances backwards only to discover that he's one stripe down. No. 8 (D3 to E5): You remember the old joke, don't you? A tiger walks wherever he wants to.

Page 20: Dutch Treat No. 1 (A2): Whoever installed the new windmill vane really goofed. Just wait till it starts turning. No. 2 (A3 to B5): Leaf peeper alert: Autumn's on its way. No. 3 (C3 to C4): That barge is drifting down the canal. No. 4 (C5): The gate arm has totally grown. No. 5 (D4): Are you sure there was a bridge here before? No. 6 (D5): Someone must have had a lot of surplus blue paint. No. 7 (E2 to E3): How do you get more space? Land fill.

Page 22: Dracula Slept Here No. 1 (A2): An arborist at work. No. 2 (B2 to C2): Some structural engineering. No. 3 (B3 to C3): Movable towers. No. 4 (B4): No need for an antenna in the digital age. No. 5 (C4): A little window remodel. The count's letting more light in. No. 6 (C4 to D4): Another case of the walking window. No. 7 (D3): Wasn't there a window there?

Page 24: Do You Buy? No. 1 (A1): More balls on the lamp for better light. No. 2 (A5): What missing beams? No. 3 (A5 to B5): Not much of a view. No. 4 (B3): Where did the sky walk go? No. 5 (B4): There's no need for a deck in this heat. No. 6 (D5): Bollard moved for a safer day. No. 7 (E1): What a beautiful lamp.

Page 26: Buzz Off No. 1 (A4): Where did that bar come from? No. 2 (A2 to B2): Flying high. No. 3 (B4): Bar none. No. 4 (D1): Do I look good in pink? No. 5 (D1): Where'd he go? That insect got hungry. No. 6 (D4): Ships do add to the seascape. No. 7 (E5): Castle in the sand.

Page 28: Head Over Heels No. 1 (A4): Who's got short legs? She's got short legs. No. 2 (B1): The building has a bad case of the stripes. No. 3 (B2 to B3): The ferris wheel wants to be center stage. No. 4 (B3): Call the rescue squad. We're one cab down. No. 5 (D1): Rubber duckie, I love you. No. 6 (E1): For want of a nail, a puzzle was made. No. 7 (E2 to E3): Freddy the seal casts a long shadow. No. 8 (E5): The boards had an urge to merge.

Page 30: Baaaah! No. 1 (A3): This cap is coming down with the spots. No. 2 (A4): The NO FARTHER sign has moved further. Nos. 3 and 4 (B2): One girl's pendant has snapped its cord, while the other girl looks like she's holding her hands. No. 5 (B2 to C3): She's wearing a matching outfit. No. 6 (B3): Her hat is off-label. No. 7 (C4): This stall is getting more than a bit board. No. 8 (D2): There are no tags on this sheep!

Page 32: The Sky's the Limit No. 1 (A5): Another aerial view. No. 2 (C2): The letters took off before this missile. No. 3 (C4 to D4): A growth spurt. No. 4 (E1): Did you know we had a base in New Mexico? No. 5 (E2): Someone scrapped that sign. No. 6 (E3): This missile woke up feeling blue.

Page 34: Where's Santa? No. 1 (A2): The antler has lost a branch. No. 2 (A5 to B5): Maybe Santa plans to radio in. No. 3 (B2): This guy gave up on Santa. No. 4 (B3): Green is more festive. No. 5 (D4): Her dress is missing some color.

Page 36: Making Merry No. 1 (A4): The cap is waving its tentacles. No. 2 (A5): It's a tall red stripe for a tall multicolored clown. Nos. 3 and 4 (B3): He's whistle-less and she's lost her hair thingie. No. 5 (C1 to D1): The balloon is a little blue. No. 6 (C3): No princesses here. No. 7 (C5 to D5): His costume leg flare is widening out. No. 8 (D1): The stuffed bunny is looking agog and wide-eyed at the goings on.

Page 38: Chillin' in Southern California No. 1 (A3 to A5): The southern lights keep shifting around, even at a zoo. No. 2 (B5): Alert, alert! There's an interloper on the ice. No. 3 (C3): Without a label, her yellow overalls just aren't designer clothes. No. 4 (C4): This guy looks like he's blushing. No. 5 (C5): He flaps for fish. No. 6 (D3): Two fish are showing off their tails.

Page 40: Olé No. 1 (A3): There's a new balcony for the ring. No. 2 (B2): The sky's the limit for this scaffolding. No. 3 (B2 to C2): Let the sunshine in. No. 4 (B3): From apples to grapes. No. 5 (C5): An unsturdy light. No. 6 (E1): The metal plate is longer.

[MASTER]

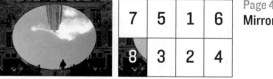

7	5	1	6
8	3	2	4

Page 43: Mirror Image

Page 44: Getting a Leg Up No. 1 (A4 to C4): The Leaning Tower of Pisa is in Italy . . . or is it? No. 2 (B1 to B2): Someone stole the flag poles. Maybe they're not very patriotic in the U.K. No. 3 (C4): Three's company. No. 4 (C5): Some of those Brits are patriotic, after all! No. 5 (D4): It looks like these swimmers have some competition. No. 6 (D5 to E5): Here's hoping that swimmer didn't drown. No. 7 (E2): She doesn't know her right from her left.

Page 46: Here's Some Moore No. 1 (A1): That's one tall tree. No. 2 (A2): What goes up must come down. No. 3 (A4): That tree was eating up too much oxygen. No. 4 (B1): Do sculptures grow? No. 5 (B2): Things are on the up and up and up and up. Nos. 6 and 7 (C3): Protect from all elements . . . or not, and could the hat be possessed? It's starting to glow. No. 8 (C4 to C5): That crate's been reinforced. No. 9 (D1): Pastel colors are his thing. No. 10 (E5): This wooden leg got lonely and joined its friends.

Page 48: Isn't It Good? No. 1 (A3): The sky is a lot more colorful all of a sudden. No. 2 (A4 to A5): Mountain climbers rejoice! Here's one you haven't climbed before. No. 3 (B3): This barn door is no more. No. 4 (B5 to C5): Now this house matches the water. No. 5 (C4): The harbor view has improved. No. 6 (D1): What a fortuitous name for a boat. No. 7 (D4): The seagull has perfect balance on top of its new buoy. No. 8 (E2): The ship's label must have gone swimming.

Page 50: Pumpkin Pilot No. 1 (A1 to A2): The shelf is a bit smaller now. No. 2 (A2): Big onions mean big tears. Nos. 3 and 4 (A3): Not only is the steering wheel singing "Let's get together and be one board," it's also casting a deeper shadow. No. 5 (A4): She's got one tall seat back. No. 6. (B1): The . . . er, headlight must have fallen off. No. 7 (B2): Now the gourds wrap around the smoke-stack. No. 8 (C3): Who replaced the yellow squash with a green one? No. 9 (C3 to C4): I don't know about you but we find this pumpkin more than a little ominous. No. 10 (D5): One of these pumpkins has lost its stem. Nos. 11 and 12 (E1): The cat is stalking the mouse, but clever mouse knew what was good for it and skedaddled. No. 13 (E5): Of course, the dog chases the cat.

Page 52: Ribbit No. 1 (A5): The right eye must see well enough to make up for the missing left one. No. 2 (B3 to B4): The frog wasn't in the mood to wear its letters today. No. 3 (C4): According to the new sign, horses might be joining the traffic jam. No. 4 (D2 to D3): The white gate is learning to hop like a frog. No. 5 (D5): The road marker is playing peekaboo. No. 6 (E4): Two lanes turn into one. No. 7 (E5): The frog got lost, looking for its princess.

Page 54: Pageantry in Prague No. 1 (A4): His hat is brim-full. No. 2 (A5): This horn is solid, man. No. 3 (B3): They must call this horse Spotty. No. 4 (B4): Quick, get the sewing kit. His uniform has popped a button. No. 5 (B4 to C4): He blows so well, they've given him a medal. No. 6 (C2): His medal is starting to turn green. No. 7 (D1): He's pulled on his high boot. No. 8 (D2 to E3): The saddle blanket is almost solid red now. No. 9 (E4): The horse's button was sold to the silversmith for beer money.

.

Page 56: Not So Grimm No. 1 (B3): Another chimney for those chilly mornings. Nos. 2 and 3 (D4): The attic wall has changed color, and there is one window less. No. 4 (C1): These vacationers must be hitching a ride home, because someone drove off with their camper. No. 5 (C5): It's sink or swim for that patch of grass. No. 6 (D4 to D5): This canoe is pea green with envy. No. 7 (E1): Quack, quack! No. 8 (E2 to E3): Did that duck get hungry and eat the paddle for dinner?

Page 58: Puppy! No. 1 (A5): In case you were thinking of lighting up, think again! No. 2 (B2): His tusk is trying to shake her hand. Nos. 3 and 4 (C5): Maybe someone's making a wish with his missing rib bone, and he may be old but he still has incredible balance, even without his femur. Nos. 5 and 6 (D2): She's training to be an air traffic director, and it's time to put away your camera phone. No. 7 (D3): A clown dropped in to brighten the day. No. 8 (E1): Rapunzel, Rapunzel, let down your long hair!

Page 60: Up, Up, and Away! No. 1 (A1): This balloon is westbound. No. 2 (B3): One of these letters is not like the others. No. 3 (C1): One balloon is awfully musical. Nos. 4 and 5 (C3): A balloon has gone wireless and lost its basket. Watch out! No. 6 (D2 to E2): This balloon park is shack-a-licious! No. 7 (D3): Up, up, and upside down! No. 8 (E1): She can't make up her mind which way to look. No. 9 (E4 to E5): Nothing can replace the mother-daughter bond.

Page 62: Spanish Panache No. 1 (A2 to A3): The crane is playing tricks on us. No. 2 (A4): A tree grows in Barcelona. No. 3 (A5): Barcelona is so eco-friendly, this tower is going green! No. 4 (B2): The house has taken a decidedly asymmetrical turn. No. 5 (B4 to C4): My, what big circles you have! No. 6 (B5): Did anyone see who used white-out on these tiles? No. 7 (C3): Can you say "pest control"? No. 8 (E2): Whoever took the red and black tile felt bad and put it back. No. 9 (E5): These tiles are not dependable. They keep changing their colors!

Page 64: Slip Slidin' Away Part of this palm tree is missing in photo No. 1. Did it decide to go for a ride before the crowds arrive?

Page 65: One Wired Pachyderm In photo No. 5, the man's new shirt goes perfectly with the elephant's recycled parts.

Page 66: A Paddle Puzzle No. 1 (A5): I can see clearly now, the cloud has gone … No. 2 (B1 to C1): There are a lot of boats on the water today. Be careful! No. 3 (B2): Wig time! No. 4 (B3): That's one long kayak! No. 5 (B4): Canopies look better in red. No. 6 (C1): Attack of the orange kayaks! No. 7 (C3): It's this way, honey. No, it's that way. No. 8 (C4): Who wants duck for dinner? No. 9 (C5): Six is an unlucky number, anyway!

Page 68: Equine Elegance No. 1 (A1): Somehow a rider broke off the tip of his flagpole. No. 2 (A2 to B2): This flag has gone crimson. No. 3 (A5): Big-eared horses hear their riders' commands better, at least

that's the theory. Nos. 4 and 5 (B2): As the lamp pole shot up seemingly overnight, the tower disappeared. No. 6 (B3): He's shy an ear. No. 7 (D1): This leg is just too much of a good thing. Nos. 8 and 9 (D3): A horse is no longer lifting his leg, and a cross has fallen off a blanket. No. 10 (E2): Walking without a hoof has got to be painful. No. 11 (E3 to E4): Who washed the saddle blanket in hot water? It wasn't shrink-free. But now it is.

Page 70: Mickey Slept Here No. 1 (A3 to B3): The electricians installed an extra overhead. No. 2 (B2 to C2): The wallpaper is double curvy here. No. 3 (C2): Mickey likes a very tall glass of water at bedtime. No. 4 (C3): No, Mickey, pink trim is actually quite masculine. No. 5 (D1): To the unknown person who took the drawer knob: if you return it, there will be no questions asked. No. 6 (D2): Mickey lost a star, or at least his shoe did. No. 7 (D3): Really, having your initial on a bed is a little ostentatious. No. 8 (E1): This just became one very long floorboard. No. 9 (E2 to E3): The way it's going, eventually the rug will be spotless. No. 10 (E5): The armoire's side panel now reaches the ground.

Page 72: Perplexing Pastoral No. 1 (A2): Welsh chimney sweeps are known for stretching their chimneys as they clean them. No. 2 (B2 to B3): Pink shutters are all the rage now. No. 3 (B3): The window is trying to match the chimney in height. No. 4 (B4): The building gained a spiral. No. 5 (B5): Where did this gargoyle come from? No. 6 (C5): Okay, now pay attention. The painting hanging inside the window had a slice taken out of it. No. 7 (D2): Two tulips volunteered for extra duty. No. 8 (D4): The arrows can't make up their minds. Nos. 9 and 10 (D5): Not only did the building lose a window, the garden statue has left the premises. No. 11 (E2): The planter now has more room to plant plants, like those two tulips above. No. 12 (E2 to E3): The shadow has been smoothed out.

Page 74: Arms Up No. 1 (A2): In Tibet, gold grows from building tops. No. 2 (A3): This flag wants to stand out from the rest. No. 3 (B1): A room with no view times two. No. 4 (B2): Things are getting a little swirly-whirly around here. No. 5 (B3): The bottom half of this building wanted to be like its top. No. 6 (B5): Good luck getting up these stairs! No. 7 (B5): It must be Valentine's Day. No. 8 (D4): Her waist tie is flying higher. No. 9 (D5): It's hip to be a purple square … or rectangle.

Page 76: Bird's Eye View No. 1 (A2): The yellow wall has a new paint job. No. 2 (A3): An enterprising home-owner has added a new skylight. No. 3 (A3 to B3): This skylight has restless window syndrome. No. 4 (A4):

Chimney Whimney had a great fall . . . No. 5 (B2 to C2): The roof is a bit edgier today. No. 6 (B4): The attic window has been bricked in. No. 7 (C2): Two windows have joined forces as one. No. 8 (D5): He's just walking along, walking along. No. 9 (E2): The sunlight is bleaching this umbrella away. No. 10 (E3): The plaza tiles have been filled in.

[EXPERT]

Page 79: Aspiring Spires No. 1 (A2): An easterly breeze. No. 2 (A5): Scramble the fighters! No. 3 (A5): They keep building them higher and higher. No. 4 (B1): Time flies when you're having fun with LIFE Picture Puzzles! No. 5 (B3 to C3): Colors of the rainbow. No. 6 (B4): Another minaret. No. 7 (C1): No more window. No. 8 (D2 to E2): Steeple, goodbye! No. 9 (E2): Be green.

Page 80: Whoa! No. 1 (A1 to B1): Having an off day. No. 2 (A4): Another pillar for good measure. No. 3 (A5): Darker nights. No. 4 (B4): Pigeon galore. No. 5 (C4): Now he's on the blue team. No. 6 (C5): Are all the guards ambidextrous or just this one? No. 7 (D1): Don't place a bet on this three-legged horse. No. 8 (D2): This horse was tired of wearing all black. No. 9 (D5): A lawsuit waiting to happen.

Page 82: London Calling No. 1 (A5): Werewolves beware when there is a full moon above. No. 2 (B1): A little more gold, please. No. 3 (B3): We thought it was taller. No. 4 (B4): The law of gravity is not in this cyclist's favor. No. 5 (C5): Where did my spire go? No. 6 (D1 to E2): Sometimes less is more. No. 7 (D3): There's a problem with the structural integrity. No. 8 (D4): Adding some light to a dark place. No. 9 (D5 to E5): Is someone expecting a baby girl?

Page 84: Kayak Attack No. 1 (A4 to A5): No more mesh. Nos. 2 and 3 (B1): A Union Jack, plus the tallest palm tree I've ever seen! No. 4 (B2): Two of these poles were fighting so a third one stepped in to break it up. No. 5 (B3 to C3): There were too many windows. No. 6 (D1): Beware of the vanishing kayakers. No. 7 (D4 to D5): They call me mellow yellow. Quite rightly! No. 8 (E1 to E2): This buoy is making a quick getaway. No. 9 (E3): Jaws! No. 10 (E5): Bananarama!

Page 86: In Gay Paree No. 1 (A2): The building has some buckteeth. No. 2 (A5 to B5): The two small blocks joined into one. No. 3 (B1): Hopefully those missing letters didn't fall on someone's head. No. 4 (B2): Candles give such a nice light. No. 5 (B4): This *E* is not making it easy. No. 6 (C1): One more support to hold up the façade. No. 7 (C2): Paris is known for its hovering lampposts. No. 8 (D1): This café needed some greenery. No. 9 (D5): Now this pole is as tall as the waiter. No. 10 (E5): It's a French thing.

Page 88: When in Venice . . . No. 1 (A1): You can never have too many statues. No. 2 (A2 to B2): Double trouble. No. 3 (A4): These are old buildings, sometimes small pillars fall off. Nos. 4 and 5 (B2 to C2): Taller + bluer = flaggier. No. 6 (B3): Reach for the stars! Scaffolding! No. 5 (B5): The builders forgot one. Nos. 8 and 9 (C3): A more contemporary window design and another steeple don't hurt the landscape one bit. No. 10 (C4): Watch out for the missing balcony. No. 11 (C4 to D4): Either this girl only has one arm, or we just can't see it. No. 12 (D4): A nonthreatening police officer.

Page 90: Morning Recess No. 1 (A1): The crane is no more. No. 2 (B3): Velazquez has a big head . . . and maybe a perm! No. 3 (C4): The decal has disappeared. No. 4 (D2): His shirt is moody. No. 5 (D2): While the kids were playing tag, this curtain crept down. No. 6 (D3): This Harry Potter protégé made himself invisible. No. 7 (D5): This way and that way. No. 8 (E5): Put your shoes on, kid!

Page 92: It Doesn't Quite Fit In photo No. 6, the passenger has no passenger handle to hold onto.

Page 93: Savory Skewers You may have a hard time figuring out the cook's name in photo No. 3. His name tag's missing.

A
N
S
W
E
R
S

Page 95: O Canada No. 1 (A3 to B3): The mountain appears to be pumping itself up. No. 2 (B3): As the mountain goes up, the roof goes down. No. 3 (B4): A street lamp has blown away. Nos. 4 and 5 (B5): As the rubberized lamp stretched out, a tree moved into the neighborhood. Nos. 6, 7 and 8 (C3): A window fled as the siren and street light poles both reached for the sky. No. 9 (C4): In a reversal of autumn, the flag's maple leaf has gone from red to green. No. 10 (C5): The light has changed. Of course, it didn't switch positions, but never mind. No. 11 (D1): His pants have lost a loop. No. 12 (D2): Repeated use appears to have misshapen this cymbal. No. 13 (D3): From Yamaha to off-label with one quick clone brush. No. 14 (E2): Never use vanishing cream on your sax. No. 15 (E2): They call him Mr. Long Legs. They just call his shadow, shadow. No. 16 (E3): This shadow's gone to that mystical place in the sky, shadowland. No. 17 (E3 to E4): The manhole doesn't need to be covered anymore—because it ain't there. No. 18 (E4): Watching a parade is a timeless event, at least once your watch has been stolen.

Page 96: The Fruity Nile No. 1 (A1): Demolition. No. 2 (A2): Who's been telling lies to make this building grow like Pinocchio's nose? No. 3 (A5): The high rise decided to get shorty. No. 4 (B2): The horizon will never be the same with that palm tree. No. 5 (B3): No need for the wood support. It's all smooth sailing. No. 6 (B4): Goodbye, banana. No. 7 (C1): Can't get enough of the color blue. No. 8 (C4): Who needs a profile when you've got so many bananas? No. 9 (C5): Turn that floating banana back around. No. 10 (D1): This banana forgot to put its Dole on today. Nos. 11, 12, and 13 (D5): A sandal fell in the water, and the boat has a design complex . . . two of them. Anchors away.

Page 98: A Dab of India Ink No. 1 (A1): There's no symbolism to the missing cymbal. No. 2 (A2 to B2): The painter has changed the background color in one scene. No. 3 (A3): Someone has lost his bird's eye view. No. 4 (A3): The scroll has been widened. No. 5 (A4): He's being examined for the medical condition of flippy legs. Nos. 6 and 7 (A5): Mr. Red and Mr. Green are now Bluemen. No. 8 (A5 to B5): Almost everyone likes yellowtail. No. 9 (B1): When all you do is sit around and meditate, you've got plenty of time for your beard to grow. No. 10 (B2): Apparently, a flower doesn't grow in India. No. 11 (B3 to C3): Someone tugged on this painting once too often and pulled it out of shape. No. 12 (B3 to C4): With a jacket this color, he must be of royal blood. No. 13 (B4 to C5): They're about to discover that, indeed, smoking can be hazardous to your health. No. 14 (C1 to C2): Puss 'n Fish. Puss 'n Fish. No. 15 (C2 to D2): Did you ever read *Painting Through the Looking Glass*? It will flip you out. No. 16 (C4): This guy needs an immediate visit from the Fuller Brush, man. No. 17 (D3 to D4): Now which do you like

better, a green or blue background? No. 18 (D4): And do you like blue or green skies? No. 19 (E2): This plant is leafing out.

Page 100: Let the Good Times Roll No. 1 (A1): When the red kite hawk goes glide-glide-glidin' along . . . No. 2 (A4 to B4): The tower had an upgrade. No. 3 (B3): But the dowel has been downsized. Nos. 4 and 5 (C2): When her bracelet gained a spiral, her other hand disappeared. No. 6 (C3): A different dowel must have fallen off. No. 7 (C3 to D3): Her wing is getting a little ragged. No. 8 (C4): The triangles have resequenced themselves. No. 9 (D1): It was time for a blue spot, wasn't it? No. 10 (D1 to D2): Her earring popped a bead. No. 11 (D4): He's having a kicking good time. No. 12 (E1): She's taking a restroom break. Nos. 13, 14, and 15 (E3): The extra lamp has illuminated the true meaning of LIFE, so let the drumming begin. Nos. 16, 17, and 18 (E5): Is that Woody behind the big-brimmed hat? If so, give him an extra star.

Page 102: Bali High No. 1 (A1 to B1): Didn't you get the blue flag memo? No. 2 (A5 to B5): That memo was followed up with one about a missing flag. No. 3 (B1): A bird carried off one of the sheaves of wheat. Nos. 4 and 5 (B2): We're up one flower and down one decorative wall scroll. Nos. 6 and 7 (B3): Now there's an extra itsy-bitsy window, while the wooden drawer has lost its stone latch. No. 8 (C1): The flagpole is clearly retreating backwards. No. 9 (C2 to C3): Now he's a golden god. Nos. 10 and 11 (C3): After the miracle of the levitating lamp, everyone relaxes with a little game of beach ball. No. 12 (C4): Someone filched her arm band. No. 13 (E1): Now we know where Chuck Berry learned how to duck walk. No. 14 (E3): He had a yellow belly band. Now he has a green one. Will miracles never cease?

Page 104: You've Got Lemons . . . No. 1 (A5): A flag, far, far away. No. 2 (B2): What will they do without their point? No. 3 (B4): A flag by any other color wouldn't blow as sweet. Nos. 4 and 5 (B5): A no-star hotel, that's totally backwards. No. 6 (C3): Another window means fewer lemons, but you probably have enough, anyway. No. 7 (D2): An open door policy. No. 8 (D3): A little jangle is missing from her arm bangle. No. 9 (D4): She's more flexible than Gumby! No. 10 (D5): sssssssssssss-up? No. 11 (E1): A green thumb added more red flowers.

Page 106: **To Kingdom, Come!** No. 1 (A4 to A5): In the Magic Kingdom, trees leaf out on demand. Or else. No. 2 (B2 to C2): Think pink! No. 3 (B3): They may have to call in Sherlock Holmes to solve the mysterious case of the missing castle window. No. 4 (B4): A new flag flies at the castle. No. 5 (C4): The Wolf must have dropped his cane while chasing Little Red Riding Hood. No. 6 (C5): Her cuff has been blued. No. 7 (D1): He likes to hummy a little tune about his hunny. No. 8 (D2): Tigger is sporting a new belly stripe. No. 9 (D2 to D3): Did you ever notice how big Pluto's eyes are? Nos. 10 and 11 (D3): Minnie's dress may be short one spot but the big news is that Mickey's got a pinkie, Mickey's got a pinkie. No. 12 (D4): And his pants have popped their buttons. Nos. 13 and 14 (E2): My, what big hands you have for a dwarf. And Goofy, what wide pants legs. No. 15 (E3 to E4): They're going to have to change Goofy's name to Gummy.

Page 108: **Water Taxis** There's a conflicting arrow in photo No. 3.

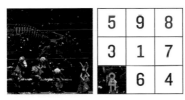

5	9	8
3	1	7
	6	4

Page 109:
String Theory
Did any of you geniuses guess that 1, 2, 5, and 8 are flipped?

[LIFE CLASSICS]

Page 111: **A Man, a Plan, a Canal**
No. 1 (B2): Let there be light! Let there be windows! No. 2 (B4): This doorway makes for a really grand entrance. No. 3 (C2 to C3): We think they call this a long boat. No. 4 (C3): It looks like the gondola's risso sank beneath the waves. No. 5 (C4): We've played a nasty trick on the gondolier and his pole. No. 6 (E1 to E5): If the water keeps rising, everyone's going swimming.

Page 112: **Foxy Business** No. 1 (A4): A chimney has been swept away. No. 2 (B5): The shingles are steadily marching down the wall. Nos. 3 and 4 (C3): A bystander waits patiently by her car as the Post Office sign drifts slowly downward. No. 5 (D1): Of course you've heard of the invisible man but this is the invisible wheel. Or it would be if the formula worked properly. As it is, it's the half-visible wheel. *Sigh.* No. 6 (D5): The dog trots freely

in the street, at least until the hunt begins in earnest. Nos. 7 and 8 (E2): A brown fetlock may blend in well with the rest of the horse but dyslexic license plates can be quite difficult to read.

Page 114: **A Parisian Poseur** No. 1 (A1): A tower is missing. What tower? Guess. You're in Paris, after all. No. 2 (B1): The lamp produces so much light, it's floating on air. No. 3 (B3): He may have ditched his glasses but it hasn't helped much. No. 4 (B5 to C5): It's another case of a missing street light. No. 5 (D3): His jacket is going to keep him just a bit warmer now. No. 6 (E3 to E4): We've heard of Big Foot, but this seems to be Big Shoe. No. 7 (E4): The fender has been snipped short.

Page 116: **To the Manor Born** No. 1 (A4): That disappearing window really has no manners. No. 2 (A5 to B5): More branches provide the hoi polloi with more summer shade. No. 3 (B3): This is what happens when a top hat becomes a stovepipe. No. 4 (E1): Beware of the shrinking waiter. No. 5 (E3): Horsey's trying its very best to curtsey. No. 6 (E5): Poor duckie is a long, long way from Golden Pond.

Page 118: **Ain't It Grand!** No. 1 (A5): The plane is backtracking. No. 2 (B3): The canyon walls are going through some tectonic uplift. No. 3 (C2): The new hat is just ridiculous on him. No. 4 (D1): One of these shadows has been scrubbed clean. No. 5 (D4): He may have copied his taste in hats from the gentleman next to him, but on him it looks good. No. 6 (E3): He's got longer legs and knockier knees. No. 7 (E5): If the safety rail loses any more bars, it won't be very safe at all.

Old and New

In Egypt, the Sphinx has company

BRUNO MORANDI/GETTY

11 changes

KEEP SCORE

3min 55sec

Can you solve the riddle of the Sphinx?

ANSWERS No. 1 (A1): They're landing in an airplane, don't know when they'll take off again. No. 2 (A1 to C2): This sphinx is getting a swollen head. No. 3 (B1 to C2): A flock of seagulls, I mean pigeons, is on the prowl. No. 4 (C3 to D3): The building has been repaired with cement. No. 5 (C5): The siren has been silenced. No. 6 (D3): I want my DirecTV, so give me back my trakking satellite dish. No. 7 (D3 to E3): Major Squab to ground control: "I'm coming in for a landing." No. 8 (D3 to D4): The shutters have yellowed over time. Nos. 9 and 10 (D4): Talk about coincidences! A window and a blue stripe have been eliminated. No. 11 (E3 to E4): The pedestal has been stretched.